TEN OF THE BEST MYTHS

MYTHICAL HERO

STORIES

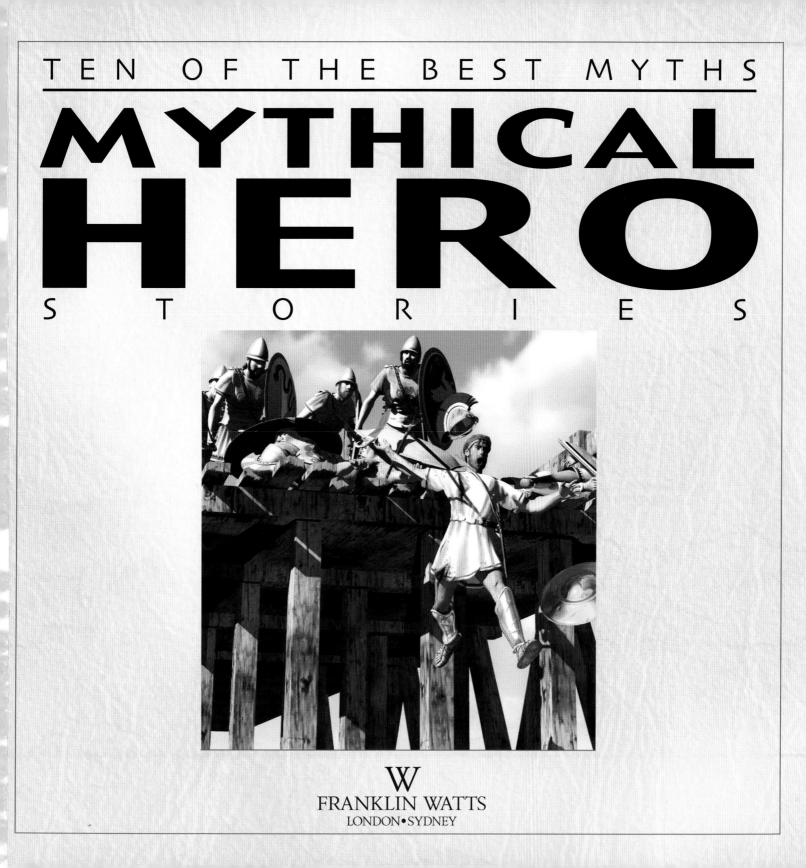

W

FRANKLIN WATTS

LONDON • SYDNEY

First published in the UK in 2014 by Franklin Watts

Franklin Watts
338 Euston Road
London NW1 3BH

Franklin Watts Australia
Level 17/207 Kent Street
Sydney, NSW 2000

Dewey classification: 398.2'1

A CIP catalogue record for this book is available from the British Library.

ISBN: 978 1 4451 3235 8

Franklin Watts is a division of Hachette Children's Books, an Hachette UK company.
www.hachette.co.uk

TEN OF THE BEST MYTHS MYTHICAL HERO STORIES
was produced for Franklin Watts by
David West Children's Books, 6 Princeton Court, 55 Felsham Road, London SW15 1AZ

Designed and illustrated by David West
Contributing editor: Steve Parker

Printed in China

THE STORIES

Theseus

Theseus, one of ancient Greece's greatest heroes, was son of Aegeus, King of Athens.

Every seven years, Athens had to send seven young women and seven young men as a tribute to King Minos of Crete. They were to be devoured by the Minotaur. This horrific beast, half man and half bull, lived in a maze, or labyrinth, made by a man called Daedalus.

On the third occasion of seven years, Theseus asked to take the place of one young man – and slay the monster. He told his father, Aegeus, that his returning ship would display white sails to show his success.

When Theseus arrived in Crete, King Minos' daughter Ariadne fell in love with him at first sight. Before the Athenians were sent into the labyrinth, she secretly passed to Theseus a sword and ball of wool.

The labyrinth, a maze of tunnels, was under King Minos' Palace of Knossos. Legend said that no one could find a way out.

Bulls and bull worship were important in Minoan Crete. Acrobats leaping over bulls were part of their religious rituals.

Theseus tied one end of the wool at the entrance to the labyrinth. He would unravel it and then be able to find his way back. As he set off into the maze, the Minotaur's terrible roar echoed through the tunnels. Theseus finally arrived at the beast's lair, strewn with human bones. Suddenly the monstrous form of the Minotaur appeared. Seeing Theseus, it let out a blood-curdling bellow, lowered its head and charged. Brave Theseus stood firm and, with one swift blow of the sword given to him by Ariadne, he killed the monster.

Theseus and the Athenian youths escaped. They fled from Crete, taking Ariadne with them.

But on his return, the hero forgot to raise white sails instead of black ones. His father saw the returning ship. Believing Theseus to be dead, Aegeus threw himself from the cliffs into the sea – the Aegean Sea.

Perseus

Perseus the ancient Greek hero was the son of Zeus, king of gods, and Danae, daughter of King Acrisius of Argos.

King Acrisius was told he would be killed by his daughter's son. So he cast his daughter Danae and her son Perseus into the sea in a chest. Washed up on the Isle of Seriphos, they were cared for by the fisherman, Dictys.

Dictys raised Perseus as his own son. Dictys' brother, Polydectes, was king of the Isle of Seriphos and wanted to marry beautiful Danae. But she had no interest in him, and her son Perseus protected her from his attentions.

One day the king tricked Perseus into promising him any gift. Polydectes asked for the head of the Gorgon, Medusa, whose stare turned people to stone. As Perseus set off on this quest, Polydectes thought: "I have finally rid myself of this troublesome son of the woman I love."

The goddess **Athena** was alarmed. She instructed Perseus to find the **Hesperides** nymphs, who had weapons to defeat the Gorgon. First Perseus had to search out the Graeae, three old women with one eye between them, since they knew the location of the Hesperides' garden. The Graeae revealed this only when Perseus snatched away their eye. Upon finding the Hesperides, Perseus received weapons and a polished shield.

At last Perseus arrived at the Gorgon's lair. As he picked his way through the stone statues of Medusa's lifeless victims, he heard a slithering noise behind him. Using the polished shield as a mirror, he saw the Gorgon about to strike. Closing his eyes, he turned around and slashed out with his sword – cutting off her head.

Perseus returned to Seriphos for his revenge. Polydectes watched him arrive. The hero held up Medusa's head and the king looked at it. He turned to stone.

Perseus eventually gave Medusa's head to Athena, who had it mounted it on Zeus' shield.

Heracles

Heracles, also called Hercules by the Romans, was the greatest of the ancient Greek heroes. His father was Zeus and his mother was Alcmene, a mortal (human).

Zeus' wife, goddess Hera, hated Heracles, who was not her son. One day she sent Heracles mad so that he killed his wife and children. As punishment, Heracles was given twelve tasks, called labours, by his arch-enemy, King Eurystheus.

Heracles was only eight months old when Hera sent two giant snakes into his room. Heracles showed no fear, grabbed a snake in each hand and strangled them.

Heracles' first labour was to kill the Nemean Lion and bring back its skin. Using his immense strength, he managed to strangle the lion. But he had difficulty skinning it, since nothing could penetrate its hide. Eventually the goddess Athena advised him to use one of the lion's own claws. Heracles returned wearing the lion's skin. King Eurystheus was so afraid he hid in a large storage jar.

Heracles' second labour was to kill the Lernaean Hydra. This many-headed serpent lived in swampy Lake Lerna. It had poisonous breath, and its blood killed anyone it touched.

Upon reaching Lerna, Heracles attacked the beast, knocking off one of its many heads. To his dismay he discovered that each time he removed a head, two grew back in its place.

Heracles asked his nephew Iolaus to help him. Iolaus suggested using a firebrand to scorch and seal the neck stumps each time a head was cut off – and the second labour was achieved.

Eventually, Heracles managed to complete all twelve of his labours.

Heracles' Twelve Labours
1. *Kill and skin the Nemean Lion.*
2. *Destroy the Lernaean Hydra.*
3. *Capture the Golden Hind of Artemis.*
4. *Capture the Erymanthian Boar.*
5. *Clean the Augean Stables in a single day.*
6. *Slay the Stymphalian Birds.*
7. *Capture the Cretan Bull.*
8. *Steal the Mares of Diomedes.*
9. *Steal the girdle of Hippolyta, Queen of the Amazons.*
10. *Steal the cattle of the giant Geryon.*
11. *Steal the apples of the Hesperides.*
12. *Capture and bring back Cerberus.*

Horatius

Horatius Cocles was an officer in the army of the ancient Roman Republic. It was the time when the army of Lars Porsena, King of Clusium, attacked the City of Rome.

As Porsena's army approached Rome, country people fled to the safety of the city. Its walls and the River Tiber provided formidable defence. Only one wooden bridge allowed access to the city across the Tiber. This was guarded by soldiers under the command of Horatius Cocles.

The panic of the fleeing people spread to Horatius' soldiers, who threw down their weapons and ran. Realising the importance of the bridge, Horatius tried to stop his men running away. But only two brave soldiers stayed with him.

Lars Porsena was an Etruscan king known for his war against the City of Rome. The Etruscans were a civilisation of ancient Italy, which eventually became part of the Roman Republic in the late 4th century BCE.

Horatius shouted to the fleeing soldiers to fetch axes and destroy the bridge behind him, while he and his two loyal companions held back the enemy.

The Etruscan soldiers attacked. The three Romans fought bravely to keep them at bay. A shout eventually came from the Roman soldiers behind: "The bridge is about to collapse!"

Horatius told his two companions to go while he continued to repel the enemy. As the Etruscans attacked again, Horatius was wounded several times. Then a portion of the bridge gave way. Knowing that the city was now safe, Horatius jumped into the River Tiber. Although wounded, and wearing heavy armour, this hero of Rome managed to swim to safety.

Lars Porsena's army lay siege to Rome. One night, a Roman youth named Gaius Mucius sneaked into the Etruscan camp to kill Porsena, but killed his secretary by mistake. When captured, Mucius said that he was just the first of 300 youths to attempt this feat – and thrust his hand into a fire. Porsena was so impressed, he quickly made a peace treaty with Rome.

Beowulf

Beowulf was a heroic warrior of the Scandinavian people called the Geats, during the late 5th century CE.

Beowulf and his men were asleep in the great hall at Heorot. They had spent most of the night drinking and singing with their host, Hrothgar, King of the **Danes**. But out in the dark, their noise tormented the giant beast, Grendel. It entered the great hall to destroy the noise-makers.

The screams of one warrior being ripped apart by Grendel, woke the rest of the men. Beowulf sprang to his feet and attacked the monster and tore off one of its arms. Grendel ran howling into the night.

The Geats were a tribe that lived in Gotland, Sweden. The story of Beowulf survives as a manuscript, written in the 8th century CE by an Anglo-Saxon poet in England.

The king and his men rejoiced, but not for long. Soon a more terrifying creature attacked the hall, killing another trusted warrior. This was Grendel's mother, come to avenge her son's death. As she left, Beowulf tracked her to her lair in a lake.

Diving into the lake, Beowulf battled the monster. But his sword broke on her back and only his well-made armour saved him from her fury. With luck, at the bottom of the lake was a mighty sword. Beowulf seized it and struck off his foe's head.

Beowulf was honoured as a hero and made King of the Geats.

Fifty years later, a golden cup was stolen from a dragon's lair. The dragon terrified the country, burning the land. Beowulf, now an old man, faced the dragon with one warrior, Wiglaf. Together they killed the dragon, but Beowulf was mortally wounded and laid to rest with the dragon's treasure.

The Maya Hero Twins

The hero twins Hunahpu and Xbalanque were summoned to the Mayan underworld, called Xibalba, by the lords who dwelled there.

The hero twins' father and uncle were famed ball-players, but they were lured to the underworld and killed by the Lords of Xibalba. Later the hero twins Hunahpu and Xbalanque caught a rat. It bargained for its life by telling them how their father and uncle had been tricked and where to find their ball-playing gear. Finding the ball-playing equipment, they released the rat and decided to have a game themselves. But the noise they made upset the Lords of Xibalba. And so the twins were summoned to the underworld for a ball game there.

The Maya civilisation existed in Central America from 2,000 BCE to 900 CE. Temples and other stone buildings are still being discovered in the jungle today.

Knowing how their father and uncle had been tricked and killed, the twins were ready to avenge their deaths. The journey to the underworld was difficult and dangerous but eventually they arrived.

Hunahpu and Xbalanque were met by the Lords of Xibalba, who set them several tests. The twins passed the tests easily – which angered the Lords. Eventually they all played a ball game. The twins beat the Lords at that too, which made the Lords even angrier.

Played in a special court by hitting a rubber ball through a stone ring, ball games were a Mayan way of settling disputes and even wars.

Knowing the Lords would never set them free again, Hunahpu and Xbalanque allowed themselves to be burned alive. But when their ashes were scattered in a river, the twins were revived. At first they became fish, then they became human.

Now the heroes had great magic. They could kill people and then bring them back to life! The Lords of Xibalba heard of this feat. They summoned the twins back to the underworld to perform the same magic on themselves.

The Lords of Xibalba allowed the hero twins to kill them. But the twins got their revenge – they did no magic and left the lords for dead.

Jason

Jason was an ancient Greek hero, famous as the leader of the Argonauts on their quest for the Golden Fleece. His father was Aeson, the rightful king of Iolcos.

Jason agreed to undertake a quest for the Golden Fleece. He knew that if he succeeded, the throne of Iolcos would be his. He gathered 50 men and set sail in the ship **Argo**. After many adventures he and his men, the Argonauts, arrived at Colchis, the home of the Golden Fleece. The fleece was owned by King Aeetes and guarded by a never-sleeping dragon.

Jason left his men on *Argo* and met with Aeetes alone. Aeetes promised to give the fleece to Jason, but only if he could perform three tasks. The tasks were difficult and Jason was discouraged.

*The goddess Hera persuaded goddess Aphrodite to help Jason. Aphrodite convinced her son **Eros** to make Aeetes' daughter, Medea, fall in love with Jason so that she would aid him.*

With the gods' help, the sorceress Medea – Aeetes' daughter – fell in love with Jason. She used her magic to help him complete the three tasks. First, Jason had to plough a field with fire-breathing oxen. But he was protected from the oxen's flames by an ointment that Medea had given him.

Second, Jason was to sow dragon's teeth in the field. These quickly sprouted into an army of warriors, ready to attack him. Jason threw a rock at one, as Medea had told him. The warrior, thinking another warrior had struck him, hit out. Soon the warriors were fighting each other. Not one was left standing.

The third task was to overcome the waking dragon. Medea had given Jason a magic potion to make the dragon sleep. As the dragon dozed off, Jason grabbed the Golden Fleece. With Medea, he headed back to *Argo* and his men.

Jason had accomplished the seemingly impossible quest for the Golden Fleece. But there were still many dangers to face before he could claim his rightful place as King of Iolcos.

Rostam

*The ancient Persian hero Rostam is famed for his Seven Trials. They occurred on a journey to save his **Shah**, Kay Kavus, who was captured by demons.*

On their epic journey, Rostam and his brave horse Rakhsh fought lions, dragons, demons, and almost died of thirst in a desert.

Eventually, Rostam arrived at Mazinderan, where the Shah and his army were held. They had been blinded by an evil spell and were guarded by Mazinderan's demon chief, Arzang. In a fierce fight, Rostam killed the Mazinderan champion, Olad. Before Olad died, he told Rostam where Arzang hid.

Persia, modern-day Iran, has had several powerful empires. The first, founded in the 6th century BCE by Cyrus the Great, spanned parts of Europe, Africa and Asia. It was eventually conquered by Alexander the Great in 330 BCE.

18

Rostam defeated Arzang in fierce combat, then returned to Mazinderan to free the Shah and his men. But he discovered that they were blind. From the Shah, Rostam learned that the White Demon had cast the spell of no sight. And it was only the blood of the demon's heart that could lift the curse. Rostam rode to the White Demon's lair and bellowed his name. From a cave the giant demon attacked, roaring and snarling. But Rostam was too quick and strong. With a mighty blow the hero struck down the demon, cut out its heart and returned to the Shah and his men. Here the demon's blood cured the spell. Some say Rostam also cut off the demon's head and wore its skull as a helmet!

Sinbad

Sinbad was a mythical sailor and hero based in the port of Basrah, southern Iraq, around the end of the 6th century CE. Stories of his seven voyages are filled with magical places and monsters. This is the tale of his second voyage.

Sinbad grew restless with his life ashore and set off on a second voyage. Through clever trading, he amassed a small fortune and headed home. His ship stopped at a deserted island to replenish stores. Taking wine and food onto the beach, Sinbad stretched his legs. As he rested beneath a tree, he soon fell asleep.

When Sinbad awoke he found, with rising panic, that the ship had gone. He was abandoned! Climbing a tree to survey the land, he saw a distant white object and made his way towards it.

The object turned out to be a giant egg that measured at least fifty paces around.

Ports in the Middle East were full of travellers and sailors with stories and tales about the Far East.

Suddenly a monstrous bird – a roc – landed and nestled over the egg. Sinbad hid in its shadow. Quickly realising that the bird was his way off the island, he tied himself to its leg with his turban.

As Sinbad hoped, in the morning the roc took off and carried him a great distance. Eventually they landed in a valley of giant snakes. As Sinbad untied himself, the roc attacked a snake and carried it away. Looking around, to his great surprise Sinbad saw the ground was strewn with giant gemstones!

Sinbad spent the day collecting as many gems as he could carry. He was little troubled by the snakes, who hid in caves, away from the rocs.

Suddenly a large slab of meat landed nearby! Sinbad remembered stories of how merchants threw lumps of meat from the valley's cliff sides, hoping gemstones would stick to them. The rocs grabbed the meat and returned to their nests. When the birds flew off again, the merchants seized the gems.

Sinbad tied himself and his gems to the largest piece of meat and lay underneath. Presently a roc arrived and carried the meat to its nest. In this way Sinbad was rescued by merchants and their ship. He returned home with a vast fortune in gems.

William Tell

William Tell is a folk hero of Switzerland during the early 14th century. He was famous for his skill with a crossbow.

Many years ago, the people of Switzerland were ruled by a cruel tyrant named Gessler. One day he had a tall pole erected in the town square of Altdorf. At the top was placed his hat. Gessler ordered that all those who passed by should bow to his hat.

But one man from the countryside, William Tell, refused to bow. When Gessler heard this, he became angry.

"Soon the whole country will follow his example, and be sure, rebellion will follow," he reasoned. He sent out a decree for William Tell's arrest.

When William Tell and his son next visited Altdorf, he was brought before Gessler. Fame of Tell's skill with the crossbow had reached Gessler's ears and so the tyrant devised a cruel plan. He ordered Tell's son to stand in the square with an apple on his head.

The crossbow was a weapon used by soldiers and hunters during medieval times. It fired a bolt that looked like a short, thick arrow.

"Shoot the apple from your son's head and you may go free," smiled Gessler. Tell replied: "Will you make me kill my son?"

"Silence! You must hit the apple with one bolt. If you fail to shoot, my soldiers will kill the boy."

The son, with faith in his father's skill, stood firm. Tell fitted a bolt, took aim, and fired. The missile hit the apple, knocking it from his son's head. The people shouted with joy. But as Tell turned away, a bolt hidden in his clothing fell to the ground. Gessler cried out, "What did you intend on doing with that?" Tell replied: "Tyrant! Had I hurt my son, this bolt was yours."

It is said that much later, Tell shot and killed Gessler, and set his country free.

GLOSSARY

Argo The ship on which Jason and the Argonauts sailed, named after its builder, Argus.

Athena The ancient Greek goddess of wisdom, courage and handicrafts.

Danes People who live in the Scandinavian country of Denmark.

Eros The ancient Greek god of love, who can make a person fall in love with whomever he chooses.

Hesperides Nymphs who tend a blissful garden in a far western corner of the ancient mythical world.

Shah Iranian name for king or ruler.

INDEX